SUMMARY OF THE 7 HABITS OF HIGHLY EFFECTIVE PEOPLE

Powerful Lessons In Personal Change

Stephen R. Covey

Effective Reads

This book is a summary and analysis and is meant as a companion to, not a replacement for the original book. Effective Reads is wholly responsible for this content and not associated with the original author in any way.

Legal Note

This book or its parts thereof may not be reproduced in any form, stored in any retrieval system, or distributed in any format by any means be it electronic, mechanical, photocopy, recording, or otherwise without any written permission of the publisher, except as provided by United States of America copyright law.

Disclaimer

All materials in this book are for educational and informational purposes only. We accept no responsibility for any effects or results obtained from the use of this material. Although every effort has been made to provide correct and adequate information, the author assumes no responsibility for the accuracy, use, or misuse of such information.

Copyright © 2021 – Effective Reads.

All Rights Reserved.

Table of Contents

Table of Contents..ii

About Stephen R. Covey..iii

Introduction...1

Habit One: Proactiveness.......................................5

Habit Two: Having The End In Mind At The Beginning
....12

Habit Three: Focus On The Important Things First .17

Habit Four: Think Win/Win..................................20

Habit Five: Knowing Is The First Step To Being Understood..24

Habit Six: Synergize...29

Habit Seven: The Saw Must Be Sharpened............32

Key Takeaways From "The 7 Habits of Highly Effective People"...36

About Stephen R. Covey

Stephen Covey was a leadership expert who was widely regarded around the world. Time magazine named him one of the top 25 most influential people in the United States. His other roles included family specialist, lecturer, organizational consultant, and author, among others. Each of these accomplishments was built on top of his solid academic background.

Covey became an enthusiastic participant in classroom debates and graduated from high school ahead of schedule. He then went on to the University of Utah, where he earned a Bachelor of Science in Business Administration before going on to Harvard University to earn an MBA in Management. He shifted his focus away from business studies and into PhD studies in religious studies.

It has been more than 30 years since the release of Covey's most popular book, The 7 Habits of Highly Effective People, which has sold more than 30 million copies worldwide since it was first published.

Introduction

Let's get one thing straight: competent individuals are not necessarily wealthy; rather, they are those who never give up hope. Always looking for methods to improve, always striving to reach a higher level of performance.

Our book synopsis is only a small piece of the reasons why you should strive to be the next "Person" whose actions will provide value to the world around you. For millennia, the world awaited the arrival of such a life-altering masterwork, and now it has.

You will undoubtedly feel regret for anything you haven't done because of laziness or a lack of ambition at some point in your life.

After hundreds of years of moral and ethical traditions that had accompanied people, Stephen R. Covey overcame these traditions by implementing a new vision that was founded on ethical and traditional ideas. That thought process resulted in a concept that was suited for the present day.

If you follow these guidelines, you can progress from being dependent on someone else to becoming independent, and then interdependent on someone else. Independence is not the end of the story.

Stephen Covey sees the need to provide a personal example from his own family's life before he can fully dismantle the first habit.

And he used this particular example to demonstrate the significance of the paradigms we employ while examining those around us.

It was only after Covey was able to stop putting pressure and expectations on his adolescent son that his connection with him began to transform.

When he embraced him for who he was and loved him for who he was That was the turning point in the boy's development, and he began to blossom as a result.

We are in a community surrounded by other humans, and we need to progress to this higher condition to maintain our well-being.

Habit One: Proactiveness

Stephen Covey tells the story of Viktor Franklin, a Holocaust survivor, to motivate us to be more proactive in our own lives. Viktor Franklin was able to carry on and find meaning in his life even during the darkest hours of humanity's history. Being proactive entails acknowledging and accepting our obligations.

You must take charge of your life in the face of all of the changes and situations that present themselves in your path. Make judgments and take actions that are always in line with your principles, rather than depending solely on the circumstances in which you find yourself at the time of decision. The following factors influence your ability to choose an answer:

Knowing oneself

To be able to comprehend your sensations and thoughts.

Consciousness

Your ability to tell the difference between good and evil.

Imagination:

For you to be able to transcend your current situation.

Choosing Your Path

For you to be able to alter your emotions and ideas as experienced by your self-awareness.

A proactive person is generally guided by his or her principles, and, in contrast to a reactionary person, she makes it a point to make her own choices, never allowing the world or others to tell her what she should do to improve her or her family's circumstances.

If you take the initiative, no one can hurt your sentiments unless you allow them to.

This is a difficult thing to embrace, particularly if you are prone to blaming others for your troubles. Once you recognize that you are responsible for your current circumstances and that you are in command of your destiny, you will be able to alter your course in the future.

One of the most effective methods to do so is to change the way you communicate with others. Make use of terminology that corresponds to your new mental world. If you find yourself using passive statements, such as "So-and-so drives me insane," it's time to quit using them.

Recognize that you are reacting inappropriately and that you are letting others influence your emotions.

Consider a more active option, such as

"I'm enabling so-and-so to completely drive me insane." "Is there anything I could do to prevent this from happening again?"

Furthermore, you should avoid using passive phrases such as "I have to do something" and instead use their active counterparts: "I want to do something."

Concentrate on the aspects of your life that you have control over, and you will become a more productive person.

To do the best we can with what we have and to quit whining about our circumstances is to be resourceful. We, on the other hand, are the only ones who can choose how we will react in response to them.

Things we cannot control are placed in what Stephen Covey refers to as the Circle of Concern. Things about which we can influence are placed in our Circle of Influence.

And being proactive entails spending more time in the Circle of Influence rather than the Circle of Concerns.

Habit Two: Having The End In Mind At The Beginning

This concept can alternatively be interpreted as "take a step back and look at the overall picture" of a project.

Stephen Covey, on the other hand, encourages you to consider every action you take and every decision you make from a greater perspective. What you need to do is think about the end of your life and how you would wish to be remembered by those who knew you.

Think about the kind of legacy you want to leave behind. Your every move is moving you closer to that goal, and you can choose how you want to be remembered daily by developing a personality.

To be successful, you must first plan and then execute your strategy. First, you must establish what you want to achieve, and then you must track all of the behaviors that will lead you to that end.

Personal leadership, expressed in the form of the question "what do I want to achieve," should come first and foremost. Afterward, your ability to manage is tested by asking yourself, "what is the most effective strategy to attain what I want?" To achieve your objectives, you must first picture the outcome of each action before carrying it out.

To do this, it is recommended that you develop your mission statement, memorize it, and record it. The beliefs and objectives that you hold are defined in this mission.

Make a list of the values and beliefs that you hold dear, as well as the larger goals that you hope to attain in your life. The mission statement serves as your constitution, a standard by which everything can be judged and evaluated. It is also your constitution.

Giving you a sense of direction and security so that you can make the best decisions possible following your values. Because of the following reasons, when you make a decision based on your principles, you become more efficient:

1. The decision is made proactively, based on your free will, rather than as a result of someone pushing you in a particular way.

2. You are confident in your decision since it is founded on ideas that have predictable long-term outcomes;

3. Making your own decision contributes to the reinforcement of your essential values.

4. You can communicate honestly with everyone involved while explaining your underlying values; and

5. You are confident in your decision, regardless of what it is; and

Habit Three: Focus On The Important Things First

This chapter is concerned with the development of leadership talents and the explanation of the distinction between management and leadership roles. We must establish our priorities before we begin working on a particular project. The four quadrants of Time Management will be discussed in detail in this section of the book.

	URGENT	NOT URGENT	
IMPORTANT	**Q1** CRISES EMERGENCIES	**Q2** PREVENTION PLANNING IMPROVEMENT	IMPORTANT
NOT IMPORTANT	INTERRUPTIONS	TIME WASTERS	NOT IMPORTANT
	URGENT	NOT URGENT	

In the first quadrant, many believe that the tasks offered should be our primary focus throughout the day because they are the most urgent and significant.

However, it is the second quadrant, which includes the activities that are significant but not critical, that you must pay attention to.

The majority of these are preventative tasks, little measures that you must perform daily in order to attain your personal development goals or to avoid anything catastrophic from taking place. If you want to be healthy, you must consume nutritious foods and engage in regular physical activity.

In the absence of such measures, disease or fat will manifest themselves as emergencies in quadrant 1.

Habit Four: Think Win/Win

This one demonstrates everyone how vital it is to listen actively while you are in a meeting and to try to do the best you can do for your business partners.

By giving them a Win/Win solution and fostering a mentality that wants to collaborate and find answers, not just make a profit, in the long term you will accomplish significant success.

If you cannot establish a win-win situation, it is wiser not to finalize the sale. So at least you preserve the relationship to a possible win-

win arrangement in the future. Win-win agreements have the following dimensions:

1. Character: is the basis of the win/win paradigm. Only when you know your ideals thoroughly can you grasp what it means to win.

2. Relationships: established based on character. Develop brand credibility over time by engaging in relationships focused on achievement on both sides.

3. Agreements: Agreements come from relationships. An understanding must be explicit and binding: intended results, rules or parameters within which results will

be reached, resources available to accomplish results, measurements to evaluate the objectives achieved, and the consequences that pursue the goals.

4. Regulatory system: for agreements to work, there must be a system to analyze and regulate them.

5. Process: A basic process must be performed to obtain a win/win agreement: The first stage is to try to see the situation from the perspective of the other by recognizing its essential characteristics and concerns. Next, we must outline the results that we

would consider a solution acceptable to both, and ultimately we should seek the agreement or new possibilities to attain these results.

Habit Five: Knowing Is The First Step To Being Understood

You have to pay great attention to what the people around you desire, and also you have to sit and ponder on their requirements rather than just be in a hurry to offer back an answer.

Soon you will find that they open up so much more and they relate to you differently.

Especially in business meetings, strive to understand what your partners require. Make things plain by asking a lot of questions and showing them your want to learn really.

Each relationship is like a kind of emotional bank account that tracks exactly how much each person has invested in it.

The stronger the balance, the higher the trust between the parties. And to establish this balance, one must comprehend the other.

That is the habit of good communication and also the most potent habit that we can put into action instantly.

Most people spend their life learning to communicate in writing or spoken form but have little training in listening and comprehending the other person.

It is rare to encounter people who listen with the aim of understanding.

People typically listen intending to respond. Hearing with empathy is a highly powerful technique that offers you the exact knowledge to work with.

Instead of screening out what the person is saying about the filter with which you see the world (or listening), you have to understand how another person sees you.

After the physical need to survive, the most crucial need of a person is to be understood and valued.

By listening empathically, you will be fulfilling that need and can then influence the other person and work together on a win/win solution.

It takes time and effort to acquire this skill at first, but the benefits are immense.

If you learn to listen in a truly active and compassionate way, you will realize that many individuals are fairly willing to open up and consider your thoughts and advice.

Habit Six: Synergize

This is a component that challenges us to deal with the difference we find in others. To try and see if we can find common ground. And maybe even to build something new and distinctive.

Synergy means that the total is more than the sum of its parts.

Synergizing then requires creative cooperation and teamwork: people with a win-win attitude who listen with empathy can take advantage of their differences to create options unavailable before.

Gathering various distinct perspectives, in the spirit of mutual respect, results in synergy.

When you have two wholly distinct points of view, you can look for a 3rd one. This alternative shows the synergy of those two ideas.

In a firm, for example, it's vital to integrate the abilities of more people. And it is also necessary to focus on teamwork to obtain greater results than if the task would have been done by a single individual.

Participants feel free to hunt for the greatest feasible option and often get new and better recommendations than the original ones.

Synergy enables you to assimilate new points of view and create excellent results by working together. But synergy is not necessary making everyone agree.

It is to extract the best of each, never equating uniformity with oneness. The idea is not to come up with a uniform solution that everyone agrees on but to come up with a unique solution that combines the best features from all the elements.

Habit Seven: The Saw Must Be Sharpened

This is the habit that, as Stephen Covey likes to say, surrounds all the other habits and makes sure you know how to take care of all your requirements.

However, people are often very busy producing (sawing the wood) to pay attention to the maintenance of their means of production (sharpening the saw).

That causes people to see themselves generating little since they have a dull saw without.

The same is true of your behavior. When your habits are not sharp, your production falls.

That is because typically maintenance does not yield huge immediate results, but it is essential if you won't want to continue sawing and even more if you want to keep your saw.

Sharpening the saw entails the design of a balanced, systemic program for self-renewal in four key areas. You should spend at least an hour each day working on them:

1. Physical dimension: involves physical exercise, nutrition, and stress management. By eating appropriately and exercising 30 minutes a day, you will be able to improve your strength and stamina. If you do not, your body will weaken.

2. Spiritual dimension: You must refresh your dedication to your ideals by examining your mission, or by prayer, meditation, or immersion in music, literature, or nature. If you do not, your spirit will be insensitive.

3. Mental Dimension: When you read, write, and plan, your mind is

sharpened. Set priorities first and work toward them.

4. Social/emotional dimension: Be compassionate and think win-win As the four dimensions are linked, everything you do to "sharpen the saw" in one will positively affect the others. At least one hour a day, every day, you should work on the four dimensions in balance, you will establish habits that will carry you through your life.

Key Takeaways From "The 7 Habits of Highly Effective People"

Highly effective people are not the passive ones, the effective ones take the initiative, they are born leaders, not bosses, or in other words, they are just proactive. Delayers usually grumble, when they reach a hurdle down the road, they'll just give up.

Leaders or active folks, however, are those who act all the time, those daring enough to take full responsibility for their own life's achievements and failures.

The leaders notice the inner power that exists inside them, that strength is paired with freedom.

For a person to consider himself as free of mind, first that individual must be able to cope with varied situations and be prepared to confront the consequences of personal choices.

Not even leaders have the power to affect the surroundings, but they are more than capable of making the best out of them.

As indicated before Covey wants you to act, but what is more vital than an active person? – Knowing when and how to go, be determined and enthusiastic when you hit barriers along the route, and modify your approach to varied settings if necessary.

Analyze your goals carefully and see if they are realistic. A large majority of the population spends a lifetime meaninglessly without having any long-term ideas, and if they have some, quite often these ideas are revealed to be pointless, unrealistic, or even destructive.

If you're like me, you probably adore and love a celebrity with all your heart (secretly or publicly).

You see them on television, covers of commercial publications, and Covey is sure that you've noticed so far that these so-called "successful celebrities" are more prone to depression and anxiety difficulties than a typical person.

Despite becoming rich and powerful, they paid a price

Efficiency is much more than achieving a goal; it is having the ability to accomplish a goal without having to pay a significant price.